A decorative dovecote dated 1641 at Hellens, Much Marcle, Herefordshire.

Dovecotes

Peter and Jean Hansell

A Shire book

Published in 2001 by Shire Publications Ltd,
Cromwell House, Church Street, Princes Risborough,
Buckinghamshire HP27 9AA, UK.
(Website: www.shirebooks.co.uk)

British Library Cataloguing in Publication Data:
Hansell, Peter,
Dovecotes. – 2nd ed. – (A Shire album; 213)
1. Dovecotes – Great Britain – History
2. Dovecotes – Great Britain – Design and construction
I. Title II. Hansell, Jean
636.9′6 ISBN 0 7478 0504 0

Front cover: *An inhabited folly dovecote containing wooden nest boxes at Nymans Garden, Handcross, West Sussex.*

Back cover: *Scale model showing a cross-section through a traditional dovecote; by King Dovecotes, East Grinstead, West Sussex.*

ACKNOWLEDGEMENTS
Most of the photographs and other illustrations have been produced by the authors, but special thanks are due to Raymond Phillips for the Bewick engravings (page 6); to Barbara Frears for the drawings of the pigeon parachute (page 5) and the dovecote interior (page 23); to King Dovecotes for the model shown on the back cover; and to the following for photographs: K. Bennett, page 14 (bottom); G. Frecknall, page 34 (bottom two); A. M. Hansell, page 37 (top); Hertfordshire County Council, page 36 (bottom right); L. A. Hill, page 30 (centre); Dr D. Kempe, page 19 (bottom right); Lane Fox, page 36 (centre); Leicestershire Museums, page 31 (bottom); National Trust, page 16 (top left); PFD Savills, page 32 (centre); Judge Nicholas Philpot, page 19 (top right); Sloman & Pettitt, page 14 (top right); Surrey & South London Newspapers, page 34 (top two); Andrew Townsend, page 37 (bottom).

Printed in Malta by Gutenberg Press Limited, Gudja Road,
Tarxien PLA 19, Malta.

Contents

A sixteenth-century woodcut of a dovecote in which the wood pigeons in the tree are fancifully shown behaving in the same way as the rock pigeons in the tower.

The pigeon and its uses

For many centuries domestic pigeons were kept in specially built houses in order to provide meat for the table, a practice that probably originated in the Middle East and was first described in Roman times. These buildings are known in England as dovecotes, pigeon houses, columbaria and culverhouses (*culver* being the Anglo-Saxon for pigeon). Although most of these structures are no longer in use, a number are still to be found in many parts of the world. Nowadays the birds' descendants throng the parks and squares of cities unconfined and, from being so useful for the cooking pot, have come to be regarded as a nuisance.

A picturesque group of nineteenth-century farm buildings at Tytherington in Wiltshire: a combined granary and dovecote alongside a coach house.

In addition to providing meat for the larder, the pigeon has played an important role in carrying messages, in both peace and war, since remotest times: the bird's unique homing instinct enables it to return to its nest from considerable distances. In the Old Testament, Noah chose a dove to send out from the Ark so that he would know when the flood had subsided. The pigeon's use as a messenger in wartime is a moving and little known epic. In the First World War the birds were housed in mobile lofts behind the trenches and were carried by the crews of tanks and seaplanes for emergency use, while in the Second World War they were routinely taken on bomber planes. Their role in the intelligence service was also important; they often accompanied allied agents when they were dropped by parachute into enemy territory.

The feral pigeons of today's cities are largely descended from the original dovecote birds whose distant ancestors were the blue rock pigeons, *Columba livia*, which inhabit the rocky cliffs of sea

Above: *A fifteenth-century woodcut showing messenger pigeons, from an edition of 'The Voiage & Travaile of Sir John Maundevile'.*

Right: *A pigeon parachute used on the Western Front during the First World War.*

coasts and inland heights in many countries. The Columba family also includes the familiar white-collared plump wood pigeon, which has totally different characteristics and is impossible to domesticate. The turtle dove is also quite distinct, belonging to another order altogether. In common usage the terms 'pigeon' and 'dove' are used interchangeably and although the resemblance between the white dove of peace and the pigeon in the street may not be obvious both birds stem directly from the blue rock pigeon.

The exotic varieties of fancy pigeon were all bred originally from *Columba livia* in many different parts of the world. Charles Darwin, who was himself a keen pigeon fancier, estimated in 1885 that there were 228 named breeds. A few examples of these include the familiar white Fantails, the acrobatic Tumblers and Rollers, the puffed-up Pouters and Croppers, the racing Homers and the large Runts, which were bred for size and were once called Roman Banquet pigeons. This culinary variety has been intensively bred for the table in Europe and in the United States.

An antique coloured print of a blue rock pigeon (Columba livia) by the Reverend Francis Morris.

5

Two studies by Thomas Bewick (1753–1828), illustrating (left) the blue rock pigeon (Columba livia) and (right) the wood pigeon (Columba palumbus).

In the kitchen

'No man need ever have an ill-provisioned house if there be but attached to it a dovecot, a warren and a fishpond wherein meat may be found as readily at hand as if it were stored in a larder. Certainly a vast pigeon and rabbit pie is a most useful standing dish in a country house both for members of the family and for chance droppers-in, and then if properly managed there will always remain somewhat to sell over and above what is consumed at home.'

So wrote Olivier de Serres in his book on agriculture and husbandry published in 1600. The living larder that he describes provided not only a contribution to the household budget but also a solution to the perennial problem of domestic catering, particularly for the unexpected guest.

In this age of convenience foods it is difficult to appreciate the valuable role played by pigeon flesh in the past, when food was scarce and monotonous, especially in the winter months. Because fodder was scarce most farm stock was slaughtered each autumn and the meat preserved by salting and smoking. Only a few animals were kept for breeding.

The numerous recipes that have come down to us, ranging from humble pigeon dumplings to the 'Grand Patty of Pidgeons Royal', illustrate the versatile use that was made of the bird in the kitchen. Not only was it eaten in the winter months, it also featured regularly throughout the year on the menus of the great households, where variety of dishes was the rule. The young 'squabs' or 'squeakers' were considered highly delectable, and even today French recipes insist on young birds being used, although in England the few pigeons for sale are generally adult wood pigeons.

Medicinal uses

In the past, the bird was valuable not only in the kitchen. Medicinally, pigeon constituted an ingredient in the superstitious and often gruesome remedies of the Middle Ages and even earlier. In Roman times, Pliny recommended the blood of pigeons as a cure for bloodshot eyes, and centuries later several maladies, including 'melancholy sadness', were supposed to be cured by applying a live pigeon cut in half to the head or, sometimes, the soles of the feet. Another remedy used the dried and powdered lining of the bird's stomach as an internal medicine for 'dysenteries'. An even less attractive mixture of bird's dung and watercress was often prescribed as an ointment for the cure of baldness and gout.

Husbandry

In addition to these uses, the dovecote itself had several other economic advantages. The cost of the birds' upkeep was negligible because they foraged far and wide in the countryside and needed supplementary feeding only when snow was on the ground, although some owners provided grain more regularly.

Apart from the need for periodical cleaning and squab collection, little custodial care was required because, once settled in the dovecote, the pigeons' inborn homing instinct would suffice. However, there is occasional mention in medieval times of a full-time keeper of the flock, known as a *columbarius*. Initial stocking of a new dovecote required special attention because the birds, being capricious creatures, were liable to desert their new home unless precautions were taken. Before allowing the pigeons to fly abroad, it was customary to confine, feed and water them within the dovecote until the pairs had mated and hatched their first brood, by which time they had generally formed a firm attachment to the place. Another precaution was to obtain the pigeons from a distant source, even from across the English Channel, as the birds would be less likely to return to their original loft.

The birds generally mate for life and are highly prolific; each pair produces two chicks about six times annually for seven years or so. During this time the parents fatten the squabs, until they are four to six weeks old, with their own regurgitated 'pigeons' milk'. An unfailing supply of squabs could thus be relied upon. They were usually culled at the age of four weeks when still covered with down and before the pin feathers had developed. At this stage the flesh was soft, juicy and fat, and without any trace of the toughness brought about by the exercise of flying. Adult pigeons were culled to remove unproductive stock and in the nineteenth century large numbers of live birds were trapped with nets for shooting matches.

The dung from the dovecote, a useful by-product, was considered very valuable agriculturally and more potent than other farmyard varieties: 'one load is worth ten loads of other dung.' In England it was recommended for growing hops and barley, and it has been used for centuries in Italy and France for vines and in Iran for melons. In the tanning industry it was employed to soften leather and in the early seventeenth century it was a major source of saltpetre for the manufacture of gunpowder.

Nothing was wasted: the feathers and down of the pigeons, like other farmyard fowl, customarily supplied the filling for pillows and feather beds and it was a common superstition that those who slept on pigeon feathers would live to a ripe old age.

Sport

Hundreds of dovecote pigeons were used as quarry in the ancient sport of falconry and, much later, in the popular pigeon-shooting matches of the nineteenth century. As many as 120 birds at a time were required for one of these matches, up to two shillings being paid for each bird. This led to much organised pilfering from the dovecotes.

Pigeon-racing still enjoys a considerable following today in many countries, especially Belgium, where it is the national sport. The highly bred and carefully trained modern racing pigeons achieve phenomenal feats of speed and endurance, giving pride and pleasure to enthusiasts everywhere. Today's racing-pigeon fancier is a combination of owner, breeder, trainer and punter; buying and selling these highly trained birds is carried out on an international scale.

The limestone dovecote at Manor Farm, Kelston, Somerset, restored during the 1980s, stands today among unused farm buildings. It is believed to have belonged to the Benedictine nuns of Shaftesbury Abbey in Dorset.

A column dovecote built in 1835 at Grittleton, Wiltshire, in a courtyard with ranges of stables, coach house and grooms' lodgings.

Sites and rights

SITES

In medieval times the choice of a site for the dovecote, whether belonging to castle, monastery, manor or farm, seems to have been fairly haphazard. Some cotes stand quite alone at a distance from the main building, often near the fishponds, while others are closer and even abut the walls.

According to writers on husbandry in a later period, several broad considerations were important in choosing the best site although there was no general agreement. A conspicuous position free from surrounding trees was thought desirable, not only because the dovecote would be clearly visible to the homing birds but also because the sound of wind in the trees, like other loud or unusual noises, was believed to unsettle them. It is clear that the pigeons were regarded as nervous and capricious creatures, liable to desert the dovecote for ever if badly upset.

Shelter from the prevailing wind was another factor in siting the dovecote and openings for the birds were often constructed so as to face south, for maximum sun. A source of water in the vicinity from which the birds could drink and in which they could bathe

An early engraving of the ancient dovecote at Garway in Herefordshire. Believed to have been built by the Knights Templar in 1326, it stands virtually unchanged today.

was thought essential. Pigeons require an abundant water supply, particularly during their annual moult in the autumn.

Although an open situation was still advocated in the eighteenth century another school of thought recommended that, of all places, 'none is more proper than the middle of a courtyard' and several plans show this arrangement. Finally, the ever present considerations of security dictated that the dovecote itself and particularly its entrance door should be within sight of the main house, 'because the master of the family may keep in awe those who go in or come out'.

RIGHTS

In Norman and medieval times the building of a dovecote was a feudal privilege restricted to the barons, abbots and lords of the manor and later extended to the parish priest. This provoked little conflict because in economic and practical terms building a dovecote was beyond the capacities of the poor. Building sanctions were, however, gradually relaxed to the extent that a visitor to Britain in the seventeenth century commented that 'no kingdom in the world has so many dovehouses'. It has been estimated that there were 26,000 in England at about that time although it is difficult to judge the accuracy of this much quoted statistic. A century or so later, no farmhouse was considered to be complete without one.

Not only were the building restrictions rigorously enforced in the early days but severe punishment was meted out to those caught stealing or killing pigeons, whether inside or outside the dovecote. The harsh penalties, coupled with the loss of pigeon meat to supplement their diet, aroused bitter resentment amongst the rural population and in France the issue has been cited as a contributory cause of the unrest leading to the French Revolution. In Britain, pigeons were a cause for complaint as late as 1800 and a tax on dovecotes was proposed in order to reduce the loss of grain due to the birds. By that time, however, pigeon-keeping was already in marked decline and the idea of any further legislation was abandoned.

Circular dovecotes

Right: *A rugged sandstone dovecote at Blackford House in Somerset, believed to date from the time of William the Conqueror. The summit oculus is now glazed and the interior contains some three hundred nests.*

Below: *The dovecote at Embleton, Northumberland, is an early example of the 'beehive' type.*

The practice of breeding pigeons for the table was common in Roman times and several writers of classical antiquity wrote treatises on the subject giving clear and practical guidance. It is thought that there may be traces of Roman columbaria in the vicinity of Romano-British villas and in some cases the archaeological evidence is suggestive. Hitherto, however, the Normans were believed to have introduced the custom to this country and the very earliest provision of housing for pigeons is still to be found in some of their castles. Excellent examples of integral nests can still be seen in the twelfth-century stone-built keeps of Rochester Castle in Kent and Conisbrough Castle in South

Yorkshire. One of the earliest detached circular stone dovecotes still stands at Manorbier Castle in Pembrokeshire, which was built around 1150. At Dunster Castle in Somerset there is a circular rubblestone example which is believed to have been built by a Norman baron at the time of William the Conqueror; however, it was altered by Benedictine monks in the twelfth century and re-roofed later, probably more than once.

The early monasteries and religious houses also built and maintained dovecotes, as did the two orders of the international brotherhood of military monks known as the Knights Templar and Hospitaller. These were founded in the twelfth century largely to protect pilgrims travelling to and from the Holy Land, but they also established hospitals for the old and sick in Britain. At Quenington Court in Gloucestershire all that remains of one of their establishments is the well-preserved gatehouse and splendid circular dovecote, believed to have been built in the thirteenth century; its two widely splayed slit windows and walls 4 feet (1.2 metres) thick serve to confirm its early date.

A very early circular rubblestone dovecote at Dunster in Somerset, thought to have been built at the time of the Norman Conquest. It contains a well-preserved potence (pages 24-5).

Above left: *The thick-walled early dovecote at Quenington Court in Gloucestershire stands on the site of an establishment that belonged to the Knights Hospitaller and is thought to date from the thirteenth century.*

Above right: *A restored, thatched dovecote with stone, flint and clunch (tough clay) walls at Westhampnett House in West Sussex.*

Left: *An elegant green sandstone dovecote at Parham in West Sussex. The door and four bull's-eye openings are neatly outlined in contrasting brick.*

At another important site at Garway in Herefordshire there is a dated, unaltered, circular rubblestone dovecote which is regarded by many as the finest ancient example in England (see page 10). A still legible inscription over the door, translated from the Latin, reads: 'In the year 1326 Brother Richard built this columbarium.' The dovecote has a diameter of 17 feet (5.2 metres), with massive windowless walls 16 feet (4.9 metres) high and nearly 4 feet (1.2 metres) thick which are encircled on the outside by a string course to deter climbing creatures such as rats. The original domed stone roof, constructed in the old castle-building tradition, has a central summit opening for the birds; the small doorway at ground level with a stout wooden door is for people. The whole appearance is strikingly rugged and impregnable, more like a fort than a farm building, and well able to have withstood the ravages of almost seven hundred years. This ancient example can be taken as the prototype of all later dovecotes. However, modifications of the basic plan, influenced by changing architectural fashion and the use of different building materials, have resulted in a great variety of design.

In England, materials for dovecote construction range from primitive mud or clay and straw, through wattle and daub, limestone and sandstone, flint, chalk,

The seventeenth-century dovecote at Ipsden House in Oxfordshire is a fine example of a flint and brick structure.

The fourteenth-century dovecote at Hurley in Berkshire stands beside an elegantly converted tithe barn that belonged to a Benedictine priory. It contains six hundred chalk nesting niches; the roof and dormer are later replacements.

timber framing, weatherboarding, granite and slate, to the later post-medieval brick and elegant ashlar stone of the eighteenth century. Their use depended on locality and period and has produced the diverse regional variations which are today's legacy: for example, the picturesque black-and-white dovecotes of Herefordshire and Worcestershire or the flint and brick ones of Sussex, Wiltshire and Oxfordshire.

Exterior modifications to the basic design were introduced at an early stage. A cupola, also known as a lantern or glover, placed over the summit opening, maintained an entrance for the birds but also protected the interior from rain. Many different shapes and sizes are still to be seen on dovecotes of all types and ages. Early cupolas were simple and constructed of stone; subsequently they became highly ornamental and were often surmounted by a weathervane or pole-and-ball decoration. These later versions were generally made of wood, possibly lead-covered, and were sometimes partly glazed but, being delicate and in an exposed position, many have disintegrated and been replaced. In some dovecotes the reduction of light and ventilation due to the cupola led to the installation of dormer windows and occasionally

At Norton sub Hamdon in Somerset the stone dovecote with cupola, buttresses and tiny dormer windows stands picturesquely beside the church. Originally it was attached to the manor house but it was enclosed when the churchyard was extended.

13

Above left: *At Faulstone House at Bishopstone in Wiltshire the tower dovecote with its flint and stone bands is believed to be a later modification of a fortified manor.*

Above right: *The remaining fortification of an earlier house is now a dovecote at Westenhanger Castle in Kent.*

Below: *A neo-Gothic folly dovecote and belvedere standing in isolation on a knoll at Sulham in Berkshire.*

windows in the main walls. At Norton sub Hamdon, Somerset, the dovecote is adorned with a Jacobean-style stone cupola and diminutive dormer windows, while at Hurley in Berkshire the gabled dormer window forms a more pronounced feature and may indeed have been a later addition.

In some dovecotes, invariably in those without a roof entrance, external openings together with alighting ledges are placed high up on the walls or in the gables. Occasionally dormer openings served the same purpose and were sometimes fitted with shutters to keep out nocturnal intruders or to confine the birds within for the purpose of culling.

Dovecotes in the form of towers with a circular base-plan date from very early times. At Sibthorpe in Nottinghamshire the 50 feet (15.2 metres) high dovecote was built in 1325 and contains more than a thousand nest holes. Early examples at Faulstone House at Bishopstone in Wiltshire and at Westenhanger Castle in Kent are believed to be remnants of fourteenth-century fortified manor houses and were probably adapted later to house the birds. In the eighteenth century, at the time when follies and landscape ornaments had become popular, an upper-storey dovecote was sometimes combined with a ground-floor garden room, as at Sulham in Berkshire and Witton Castle in Durham.

The pretty three-stage battlemented dovecote of coarse ashlar sandstone at Witton Castle, Durham, houses pigeons in the upper two storeys.

Right: *The timber-framed dovecote at Wichenford Court in Worcestershire is today well preserved under the care of the National Trust. The interior contains unusual arched wooden nest-box openings.*

Far right: *The dovecote at the White House, King's Pyon, Herefordshire, which housed five hundred pigeons in its upper loft.*

Square and rectangular designs

Over the centuries, most square dovecotes were built to unpretentious designs, but even these run-of-the-mill examples follow the general rule that no two dovecotes are identical in every detail; the cupolas in particular allowed great scope for individual variation. Until the end of the seventeenth century, when the use of brick had become widespread for humble domestic dwellings and farm buildings, many square and rectangular dovecotes were built of stone, but the timber-framed, so-called black-and-white or magpie varieties, chiefly found in Worcestershire and Herefordshire, are among the most attractive of this group. Several have survived and restoration by the National Trust at Hawford Grange and Wichenford Court in Worcestershire has provided two excellent seventeenth-century examples. However, not all are in such a good state of repair. The earliest timber-framed, and probably the sole remaining, cruck-built dovecote stands at Glebe Farm, Hill Croome, Worcestershire. It dates from the fifteenth century and is now owned by the Avoncroft Museum of Buildings, Bromsgrove, Worcestershire. It was dismantled and repaired at the museum before being re-erected on its original site.

The Butt House at King's Pyon carries the date of 1632. Pigeons were recorded as being housed in the upper loft in 1920.

15

Above left: *A square, timber-framed dovecote at Moat Farm, Dormston, Worcestershire. The original roof would have been four-gabled like the cupola. Restored and owned by the Avoncroft Museum of Buildings.*

Above right: *The fifteenth-century dovecote at Hill Croome, Worcestershire, is probably the only cruck-framed example in Britain. It was sympathetically restored by the Avoncroft Museum of Buildings at Bromsgrove and re-erected on its original site.*

Left: *A finely reconstructed dovecote from Haselour Hall, near Lichfield, which stands in the Avoncroft Museum of Buildings, Bromsgrove, Worcestershire. Originally timber-framed, it is now clad in brick but contains wooden nest boxes (see page 25).*

Below left: *The small timber-framed dovecote at Pump House Farm, Hanbury, Worcestershire, has a plinth of coursed red bricks, which also form the infilling between the timbers (see page 25).*

Below right. *This sixteenth-century dovecote at Pimp Hall, Chingford, is probably the sole remaining timber-framed dovecote in Essex. It has been restored.*

Above: *The large, four-gabled stone dovecote at Fiddington Manor, Gloucestershire, carries a plaque with the date 1637 on an upper wall. It contains more than a thousand nest niches.*

Right: *The restored stone, four-gabled dovecote at Carswell Manor, Oxfordshire, believed to date from the early seventeenth century, contains some six hundred nest holes.*

Below left: *In Eardisland, Herefordshire, villagers saved the two-storey Manor House dovecote that had been neglected for years. It opened to the public in September 1999.*

Below right: *The brick, four-gabled dovecote at Pigeon House Farm, Eldersfield, Worcestershire, bears stone sundials on two walls and a Latin inscription: 'Now it's mine, then it's his, after that I know not what.' The upper storey has two openings in the gables for the birds.*

The typical four-gabled dovecotes are characteristic of the Cotswold tradition and some are still standing in Gloucestershire and elsewhere. A plain, square, one-storey design is most common; the large, rectangular, six-gabled variation at Lower Slaughter is unusual.

Very large rectangular dovecotes with room for more than three thousand birds include the two-chambered examples at Newton in the Willows, Northamptonshire, and at Willington, Bedfordshire, where the spectacular

Above left: An unusual dovecote at Godminster, Somerset, in which the four small main gables are matched by the cruciform gablets of the wooden louver. There are mullioned and transomed triple openings for the birds in the gables.

Above right: The large, six-gabled, two-chambered stone dovecote at Lower Slaughter Manor in Gloucestershire is believed to be the largest in the county. Note the early dripstones over the openings and door and also the string course to discourage climbing predators.

Left: The base-plan of the large limestone dovecote with red brick dressings at Brightwell Park, Brightwell Baldwin, Oxfordshire, is in the form of a Greek cross.

dovecote built by Cardinal Wolsey's Master of Horse, Sir John Gostwick, in 1530 is kept in excellent repair by the National Trust. It is notable for its crow-stepped gable roof which uniquely resembles the so-called 'lectern' type so common in Scotland and parts of the south of France. The most unusual of these large dovecotes was the enormous cruciform one at St Pancras Priory at Lewes, East Sussex, which held more than six thousand birds. Engravings show that it resembled a parish church in shape and size; it was demolished in the nineteenth century. A smaller surviving example in the form of a Greek cross is to be found in parkland at Brightwell Park, Oxfordshire. This attractive eighteenth-century dovecote is built of local limestone and has brick dressings to the quoins, windows and door.

The spectacular two-chambered dovecote at Willington, Bedfordshire, with crow-stepped gables contains more than 1300 nests. It was built in 1530 by Cardinal Wolsey's Master of Horse and stands close to the stables.

Above left: *Several square limestone dovecotes with crow-stepped gables are to be found around St Asaph in Denbighshire. At Faenol Fawr, Bodelwyddan, the four-gabled building has been re-roofed.*

Above right: *The dovecote at Queniborough Hall in Leicestershire, which was restored in 1987, displays the date of 1705 in raised bricks on the outer wall. Brick finials decorate the roof features.*

Left: *The hipped roof and ridge gablet on this dovecote in Suffolk are characteristic of the region. The primitive interior contains nest boxes of wattle and daub.*

Below left: *The seventeenth-century red brick dovecote at the Manor House, Gamlingay, Cambridgeshire, has a pyramidal roof surmounted by a louver of four small gablets.*

Below right: *The square stone dovecote with bull's-eye flight holes and contrasting quoins and dressings at Weetwood Hall, Wooler, Northumberland. It is designed to house pigeons above and chickens beneath.*

19

Octagonal dovecotes

The square and rectangular plan gradually became outmoded during the seventeenth and eighteenth centuries in favour of an octagonal, occasionally hexagonal, design. Some of these later versions have been described as dovecotes dressed up as garden ornaments, less flatteringly as 'pretentious cotes'. However, at a time when the custom of breeding pigeons for the table was already in decline, they combined elegance with utility to a remarkable degree. Stone construction was sometimes used, but building with brick in the classical style predominated. Although many of these brick dovecotes are quite plain, others have recessed panelling, diaper patterns in contrasting bricks, or dentil

Left: *The dovecote at Buckland Park in Oxfordshire is in neo-Gothic style. A vermiculated frieze separates the blind pointed arches on the ground floor from the crosslets and quatrefoils on the upper floor.*

Below left: *The hexagonal Gothic-style brick dovecote at Brocton Hall in Staffordshire now stands in the grounds of a golf club. It has an attractive cornice and recessed brick decorations.*

Below right: *The large, octagonal dovecote at Shobdon Court in Herefordshire once stood in the grounds of an earlier house. It has a pedimented doorway dated 1824. An outer staircase leads to the upper pigeon house with storage below. The interior nest holes have individual flat brick landing ledges (see page 23).*

or saw-tooth cornices. The combination of brick with other materials contributes a great deal to the charm and variety of many octagonal dovecotes. One of the most striking contrasts is with flint; several buildings embellished in this way have survived. In Sussex, where flint occurs naturally, an element of 'neighbourly imitation' may account for the number of dovecotes in this style.

Several octagonal ashlar stone dovecotes grace the grounds of elegant eighteenth-century houses in the West Country. Three handsome, well-preserved examples, all built about 1730 and each markedly different in design, provide excellent illustrations. In Gloucestershire, the dovecote at

A group of three octagonal Sussex dovecotes of flint with brick dressings: (right) Coombe Place, Pycombe; (below left) Bailiffscourt, Climping; (below right) Newtimber Place, Hassocks.

21

Above left: *At Loxley Hall, Staffordshire, all that remains of the main house (demolished in the 1960s) is the stable-yard, clock tower and the two-storey dovecote. The birds enter through the partially glazed windows below the eaves.*

Above right: *The dovecote at Frampton Court, Frampton on Severn, Gloucestershire, is an example of a group of octagonal ashlar stone dovecotes built in the eighteenth century. It contains about five hundred nesting niches.*

Frampton Court is in restrained classical style and consists of one tall storey only, whereas the Painswick House dovecote has two storeys, the lower one forming an arcaded summer house. In Bath, the three-storey Widcombe Manor Farm dovecote might be considered the quintessence of all others in terms of elegance and ingenuity of design. Each of the two lower floors are garden rooms and contain fireplaces, while pigeon nesting places are fitted not only within the top storey but are also found in equal numbers on three of the exterior walls of the middle stage.

Above: *An octagonal ashlar stone dovecote in the classical style at Painswick House, Gloucestershire. It features a square summer house below.*

Right: *A striking three-storey octagonal dovecote of ashlar Bath stone at Widcombe Manor Farm, Bath, Somerset. The two lower floors are garden rooms connected by an inner spiral staircase. The pigeons are housed in the upper loft and also in rows of external nest holes on three of the walls.*

Interior design

The inside of a large dovecote can be a most remarkable sight. The walls of the dimly lit, cavernous interior are lined from top to bottom with row upon row of nest holes, often as many as a thousand or more. Each unit is generally L-shaped to left or right or otherwise enlarged 'so that your bird sits dark and private'.

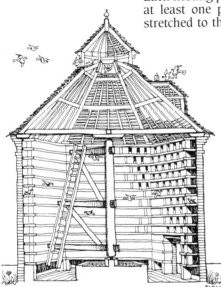

Each nesting place had to be large enough to accommodate at least one parent and two chicks but was sometimes stretched to the limit when eggs were being incubated by the hen bird at one end while chicks were being fed by the cock at the other; such was the rapid breeding cycle of the bird. For this reason, overstocking the dovecote with birds was to be avoided and the provision of three niches for every two pairs was often recommended.

Continuous ledges running below the tiers were sometimes provided for each row, less generously for every other row, or even more distantly spaced. Some dovecotes even have an individual landing stage for each hole. These projections served both for the birds to alight upon and as footholds for those collecting eggs and squabs. In those dovecotes without any ledges, deep claw marks on the brick or stonework are testimony to the birds' difficulties in entering their nests.

Above: *Anatomy of a typical dovecote. Note the central potence mounted on a low plinth, the small doorway, the dormer window and the flight entrance beneath the cupola.*

Right: *The interior of the tun-bellied or beehive dovecote at Dirleton Castle, East Lothian. A characteristic northern type, it contains more than a thousand open nesting cells.*

Far right: *The whitewashed brick interior of the dovecote at Shobdon Court contains almost five hundred nest holes, each with its own brick alighting ledge (see page 20).*

Some of the 1500 wooden nest boxes with arched openings and a potence ladder at Hall Farm, Wenden Lofts, Essex.

Matching materials were generally used for exteriors and interiors, so that wooden compartments and ledges are fitted in timber-framed dovecotes, while clay, stone and brick are used in others. In some districts chalk from inland or coastal sources was employed and, more rarely, granite or slate. In later dovecotes the rows of nest holes frequently start 3–4 feet (0.9–1.2 metres) from the floor, probably to reduce the threat from agile rats.

An ingenious contrivance known as a potence, from the French term meaning a gallows, was an early labour-saving device. These were generally fitted to circular dovecotes but occasionally to other forms; several are still to be found intact. The structure consists of a central stout wooden pole, pivoted above and below. One or two ladders were attached to lateral arms, the whole assembly rotating to provide convenient access to the nests at all levels. Sometimes useful platforms were attached to the pole for

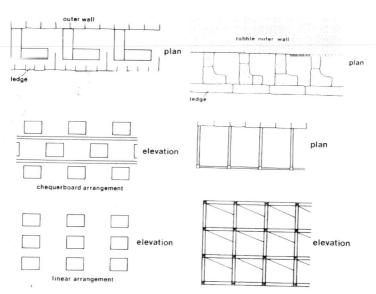

The construction of interior nesting places frequently follows that of the fabric of the structure: brick-built nests in brick buildings; stone, chalk or clunch where these materials are available; wooden nest boxes in timber-framed cotes.

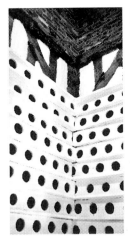

Far left: A reconstructed dovecote at Avoncroft Museum of Buildings, Bromsgrove, Worcestershire, contains wooden nest boxes with unusual circular entrances. The timber framing (above) is now obscured on the outside by brick cladding (see page 16).

Left: The interior of a dovecote is revealed in this roofless ruin at Manor House, Piddletrenthide, Dorset. Each row of brick-built nests is inset with a ledge of slate.

Left: Trelliswork wooden nest boxes are fitted to the walls of the timber-framed and brick dovecote at Pump House Farm, Hanbury, Worcestershire (see page 16).

various purposes. The potence at Dunster in Somerset is said to be four hundred years old and still moves at the touch of a finger. Square and rectangular dovecotes did not lend themselves to this arrangement and instead occasionally contained a scaffold of beams close to the walls which was reached by ladder and provided walkways.

Whenever it was necessary to confine the birds within the cote, an interior trapdoor below the cupola could be operated from inside or outside, either by means of a rope and pulley or by hand using a fixed peg ladder to make the ascent.

Unusual interior features, all circular in shape and placed in the middle of the floor, include: a stone column with projecting spiral steps as at Penmon Priory, Anglesey; a raised platform containing an extra twenty-two nest holes and into which the base of a potence is inserted at Whitton Hall, Shropshire; and a stone basin with water supply at Garway, Herefordshire.

The comfortable interior of a converted dovecote at Church House, Bibury, Gloucestershire. Decoy pigeons peep from some of the wall niches.

John Wood the Elder of Bath designed Belcombe Court in Wiltshire in 1723 and was probably responsible for the fine ashlar domed dovecote which surmounts an arch beside the house.

Architectural fancies

The earliest dovecotes were designed for practical purposes and built according to local tradition, with little architectural pretension. It was not until the eighteenth century that their ornamental aspect was exploited, some even being sited in the newly fashionable landscaped gardens of the day. During this period it was common practice to disguise utilitarian buildings of all sorts with an elegant façade and incorporate them as eyecatchers within the grounds.

Many of these later dovecotes were constructed by local builders, sometimes supervised by their patron with pattern book in hand, but there are several still in existence which were

An elegant dovecote and stable in the form of a classical temple at Barrington Park in Gloucestershire provide a decorative landscape feature.

designed by well-known contemporary architects. For example, in 1723 John Wood the Elder designed the elegant Palladian house known as Belcombe Court in Wiltshire and is believed to have also been responsible for the unusual and imposing dovecote in the open courtyard which presents a striking counterbalance to the front elevation of the house. It is unusual to find a dovecote forming such a prominent feature in the architectural composition, but John Wood may have been influenced by some of Palladio's designs for country villas in northern Italy. In several of these, elegant pigeon houses are situated equidistantly, often as paired pavilions, on either side of the main house, to which they are connected by arcades.

In the same period an impressive dovecote and stable were disguised as a classical temple at Barrington Park in Gloucestershire. It stands at a focal point in the landscaped grounds and was clearly intended as decoration as well as a source of birds for the table. The mansion, the layout of the parkland and the dovecote have been attributed to either William Kent or William Smith of Warwick.

During the eighteenth century the Gothic Revival style became increasingly popular, rivalling the classical trend. At Wroxton Abbey in Oxfordshire, Sanderson Miller designed several features in the park, including a dovecote, folly and temple, a lake and cascades, of which only the dovecote remains. It is stone-built in the form of an octagonal battlemented tower complete with arrow-slit windows and quatrefoil decorations and is surmounted by a handsome locally wrought weathervane.

Although there was a general decline in the use of dovecotes towards the end of the eighteenth century, the building of a few new ones continued; among these are some with architectural connections. At Madresfield Court, Worcestershire, the large circular brick tower

Above left: *At Plas Kinmel, Denbighshire, the model dairy and home farm with a tower dovecote on one corner were designed by W. E. Nesfield in the 1870s.*

Above right: *This late-nineteenth-century garden folly dovecote in neo-Gothic style at the Seigneurie of Sark, Channel Islands, has flight holes dotted about its outer wall.*

dovecote was restored and embellished by Norman Shaw in 1867. His unusual commission included the addition of a large stone panel which is mounted high up on the wall above the door and dominates the building. Described as a 'château dormer', it contains rows of flight holes and a two-light window. Another grand Victorian house, Kinmel Park in Denbighshire, was built in the late 1870s. The architect, W. E. Nesfield, also designed Plas Kinmel in the grounds of the mansion as an ornamental model dairy and home farm which includes a circular tower dovecote with a striking timber dormer on stone brackets. Another idiosyncratic design was built in this period at Bemerton Farm, Wiltshire. This circular tower dovecote is on a much smaller scale and forms part of a group of outbuildings which were made to resemble a Russian farm and have ragstone walls. The dovecote is two-storeyed; it houses poultry on the ground floor and pigeons above.

The curious ragstone-walled farm buildings at Bemerton Farm in Wiltshire include a striking multi-purpose dovecote, which houses pigeons above and hens below.

Rows of pigeon holes in the white wooden gable of two of several cottages at Blaise Hamlet model village, near Bristol, built by the Regency architect John Nash.

A dovecote designed by Sir Edwin Forbes illustrated in Gertrude Jekyll's book on garden ornaments in 1918.

By the beginning of the twentieth century the function of dovecotes as broiler houses had become largely outmoded, but having one in the garden seems to have persisted as a lingering tradition and a few were still being built. Gertrude Jekyll, in her book on garden ornament, did much to encourage the trend by illustrating several contemporary dovecotes, including the one that still stands at Pednor Farm, Buckinghamshire. It was designed by Sir Edwin Forbes in 1912 at the same time as he converted the surrounding farm courtyard into a comfortable house. These modern dovecotes are all much smaller than their predecessors and were generally intended to house only a handful of fancy pigeons.

29

Far left: *An imposing entrance gateway to a model farm at Woodlands Park, Stoke d'Abernon, Surrey, surmounted by a pigeon loft with elaborate cupola.*

Left: *In the timber-framed Elizabethan stable-range at Ightham Mote, Kent, the dovecote above the entrance arch is all that remains of the quadrangular forecourt which once formed the original approach to the house.*

Courtyards and farm buildings

From the eighteenth century onwards, when fewer pigeons were being bred for food, there was a trend towards grouping farm buildings together in neat layouts often arranged to form a courtyard. Dovecotes often stood in the centre of yards, but they sometimes terminated a separate range and occasionally

surmounted an entrance arch. A brick octagonal dovecote built in the nineteenth century in Tudor style stands in the middle of an outer court formed by a barn, dairy range, chapel and gatehouse at Cockfield Hall at Yoxford in Suffolk. By contrast, the dovecote at Chetwynd in Shropshire stands quite separately from the architecturally matching stable block, while at Crossrigg Hall in Cumbria the dovecote is attached to a row of piggeries.

Above: *The stone dovecote at Crossrigg Hall, Bolton, Cumbria, includes several distinctive classical features. It is attached to the end of a row of piggeries and is part of a more complex courtyard.*

Right: *The impressive octagonal, brick dovecote at Cockfield Hall, Yoxford, Suffolk, with battle-ments and pinnacles. It stands in the middle of an outer courtyard of matching brick buildings.*

Above left: At Stadhampton, Oxfordshire, the thatched octagonal granary with icehouse below is paired with an octagonal dovecote with diaper-patterned walls and an unusual circular interior. Together with two gate piers, these are the remains of Ascott Park, dating from 1666.

Above right: This granary with pigeon loft above at Wyke Farm, Gillingham, Dorset, is mounted on traditional staddle stones. Openings for the birds are to be seen over the upper window and door.

Left: The ornamental dovecote with upper-storey pigeon loft and open arcaded ground floor stands in a meadow across the road from Chastleton House in Oxfordshire.

In early times the dovecote and granary often stood alongside each other in the farmyard. A variation of the theme is found at Stadhampton in Oxfordshire, where the octagonal brick dovecote is paired with a thatched granary, both remnants of Ascott Park, which dates from 1666. The concept of a combined granary and dovecote dates from the end of the eighteenth century, when increased yields of grain meant that additional storage had to be provided. At Wyke Farm, at Gillingham in Dorset, a dovecote granary standing on staddle stones still contains several nest boxes in the upper storey.

Outside the farmyard, shelter for livestock was sometimes provided as a loggia around a dovecote. At Swallowfield Park in Berkshire the cattle shelter which encircles the dovecote was a later addition, while at Exton Park in Rutland the elegant octagonal block for pigeons has only a partial loggia. At Chastleton House in Oxfordshire the stone two-storey dovecote has large circular flight holes for the upper chamber; the open

The central octagonal dovecote at Exton Park, Rutland, is crowned with spirelets and is partially encircled with a ground-floor loggia for livestock.

31

At Bunny in Nottinghamshire the end wall of this brick-built outbuilding has row upon row of nesting holes, the lowest tier being finished off with attractive corbelling.

arcaded ground floor serves as a shelter for livestock.

Sometimes tiers of nest holes together with alighting ledges were built into the whole or larger part of an exterior wall, as for example at Bunny in Nottinghamshire. Occasionally an outside and inside arrangement exists in which niches are located in the external wall of a dovecote with the usual complement of nest holes located internally. Fine examples are to be found at Hygga Farm in Monmouthshire and at Widcombe Manor Farm and Southstoke Farm, both in Bath.

At Burlton Hall, Shrewsbury, Shropshire, the dovecotes and various attached outbuildings have chimney-like finials and dentil cornices and are fitted with rows of nesting niches in the outer walls.

In a fine row of barns at Southstoke Farm near Bath, the end dovecote has exterior nesting holes in addition to the more conventional arrangement inside the upper storey.

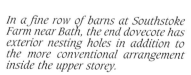

32

Arlingham Court, Gloucestershire: listed building or listed ruins? Possibly a step too far.

Ruins, repairs and innovations

Innumerable dovecotes have been lost over the past two hundred years or so and it is only recently that recognition of their worth and historical significance has grown. The Monuments Protection Programme, introduced by English Heritage in 1984, instituted a county-by-county assessment of dovecote sites in England. Their 1995 report was based on information from the Sites and Monuments Record and other sources and is to be followed by site evaluation and protection. In 1995 the total number of dovecotes was assessed as 2059, far fewer than the oft-quoted, but much disputed, figure of 26,000 thought to have existed in the seventeenth century. Today, national amenity bodies such as English Heritage, CADW in Wales and the National Trust, together with local authorities and local building preservation trusts, have an important role in both promoting and assisting in the conservation of these lesser buildings. This is an encouraging development.

Since 1980 several impressive dovecote restorations have been completed in different parts of Britain. These include the stone tower dovecote at Gatton Bottom in Surrey, which is believed to date from the fourteenth century; it stood on land occupied by Merstham railway station and was moved to its present site in 1838. At Hygga Farm, Trelleck, Monmouthshire, the circular sandstone dovecote is believed to have once been part of an abbey farm. Its unusual combination of interior and exterior nesting

Above and right: *A stone tower dovecote with Gothic features believed to date from the fourteenth century at Gatton Bottom in Surrey. Having been neglected for years and further damaged in a storm, it was well restored in 1982.*

Above and right: *The roofless and neglected sandstone dovecote with exterior and interior nest boxes at Hygga Farm, Monmouthshire, was restored in 1991.*

holes and its roof have been sympathetically restored. In Herefordshire a dramatic restoration of the charming miniature timber-framed dovecote at Luntley Court, dated 1675, was carried out in 1989. In Lincolnshire and Nottinghamshire the architect John Severn supervised the repair of no fewer than sixteen dovecotes during his lifetime; under his direction, the ruin at Dovecote Farm, Wainfleet St Mary, near Skegness, was faithfully repaired. Other successful restorations include those at Eardisland, Herefordshire, and Hangleton Manor, Hove, and several under the aegis of the Norfolk Dovecote Trust.

Left and below: *The dilapidated and shored-up timber-framed dovecote, dated 1675, at Luntley Court, Herefordshire, was restored in 1989.*

Below left and below right: *The ruined dovecote at Dovecote Farm, Wainfleet St Mary, Lincolnshire, was restored in 1991 under the direction of the late John Severn.*

Left: *An immaculate restoration at Winterbourne Court, Bristol, by a specialist builder, included the replacement of the door and window; the cupola, which had been missing since 1900, was also replaced.*

Above left: *This Sussex dovecote with coarse flint walls and chalk interior nests at Hangleton Manor, Hove, was roofless and its walls had collapsed. Its painstaking restoration using local volunteers involved the construction of a new 'penthouse' louver and interior potence ladder.*

Below: *A typical seventeenth-century four-gabled dovecote at Coln St Aldwyns, Gloucestershire, has been converted to a deceptively spacious dwelling.*

Below left: *This dovecote at Allington Castle in Kent is one of a pair built of Kentish ragstone in the twelfth century. It served as an oasthouse before being converted to a dwelling in the twentieth century. The conical tiled roof conceals the original inner stone vault.*

Below right: *The octagonal dovecote at Amwellbury in Hertfordshire, sympathetically converted for residential use by Hertfordshire County Council.*

A small modern ornamental dovecote stocked with white doves at the Goodwood Park Hotel and Country Club in West Sussex.

Several of the more substantial dovecote buildings have been successfully converted for use as dwellings. Square dovecotes seem to be the preferred shape but the octagonal cote at Amwellbury in Hertfordshire, converted in 1991, is decorative as well as useful. Other notable examples are to be seen at Coln St Aldwyns in Gloucestershire and Allington Castle in Kent. Nor has the concept of building new dovecotes died out, although these tend to be designed as decorative features rather than utilitarian structures. Two such buildings are to be found at Goodwood Park Country Club in West Sussex and Westcote Manor in Warwickshire. where the dovecote was erected to commemorate the new millennium.

A millennium belvedere dovecote at Westcote Manor in Warwickshire. Flight holes for the birds are provided in the dentil cornice.

Further reading

Ariss, P. 'The Dovecotes of Gloucestershire'. *Journal of the Historic Farm Buildings Group*, volume 6, 1992.

Beacham, M.J.A. 'Dovecotes in England: An Introduction and Gazetteer'. *Transactions of the Ancient Monuments Society*, volume 34, 1990.

Buxbaum, Tim. *Scottish Doocots*. Shire, 1987.

Cooke, A.O. *A Book of Dovecotes*. T. N. Foulis, 1920. Classic study; out of print but obtainable through libraries.

English Heritage. *Dovecotes: Monument Protection Programme Report*. 1995.

Hansell, J. *The Pigeon in History*. Millstream Books, 1998.

Hansell, P. and J. *Doves and Dovecotes*. Millstream Books, 1988.

Hansell, P. and J. *A Dovecote Heritage*. Millstream Books, 1992.

Hill, L.A. 'For the Wings of a Dove'. *Cumbria Life*, November/December 1994.

Jeevar, P. *Dovecotes of Cambridgeshire*. Oleander Press, 1977.

McCann, J. *The Dovecotes of Suffolk*. Suffolk Institute of Archaeology and History, 1998.

Peterkin, G.A.G. *Scottish Dovecotes*. Wm. Culross, Coupar Angus, 1980.

Pridham, J.C. *Dove and Pigeon Cotes in Worcestershire*. County Planning Department, Worcester, 1974.

Severn, J. *Dovecotes of Nottinghamshire*. The Cromwell Press, 1986.

Simms, Eric. *The Public Life of the Street Pigeon*. Hutchinson, 1979.

Smith, Donald. *Pigeon Cotes and Dove Houses of Essex*. Simpkin Marshall, 1931. Classic study; out of print but obtainable through libraries.

Stainburn, I.R. *A Survey of Dovecotes in the Old County of Herefordshire*. Planning Department, Hereford and Worcester, 1979.

Thomas, Michael. *Dovecotes*. National Trust (Severn Region) and Avoncroft Museum of Buildings, 1980.

Whitworth, A. *Dorset Dovecotes*. Culva House Publications, 1988.

At Hawley Manor in Kent one of the dovecote's Dutch-style dormer windows bears the date 1556 but there is some doubt about its authenticity. The most prominent feature is the unique ogival cupola, which suggests an influence more oriental than Dutch. The interior has an unusual arrangement of wall walkways and a peg ladder.

Places to visit

Below is a list of places at which typical dovecotes may be seen without difficulty. Some are designated for public access; others may be safely approached by road or public footpath without trespassing. If a dovecote is illustrated in the book but is not listed below written permission to visit must be sought in advance. Intending visitors to other sites should ascertain dates and times of opening before making a special journey. Abbreviations used are: (EH) English Heritage; (NT) National Trust; (CADW) Welsh Historic Monuments. National Grid map references are given where they may be helpful; they are included by permission of the Controller of Her Majesty's Stationery Office. An asterisk* indicates a dovecote illustrated in the book.

Abington Park, Northampton. Giant tower in public park.
*Allington Castle**, Maidstone, Kent. Telephone: 01622 54080. Carmelite friary. Pair of dovecotes.
Antony House, Torpoint, Cornwall PL11 2QA (NT). Telephone: 01752 812191.
Athelhampton, Athelhampton, Dorchester, Dorset DT2 7LG. Telephone: 01305 848363. Website: www.athelhampton.co.uk Fifteenth-century dovecote.
Avebury, Wiltshire (NT). Telephone: 01672 539250. Sarsen stone dovecote and pond by the Alexander Keiller Museum and the Great Barn Museum of Wiltshire Folk Life.
*Avoncroft Museum of Historic Buildings**, Stoke Heath, Bromsgrove, Worcestershire B60 4JR. Telephone: 01527 831363 Website: www.avoncroft.org.uk Meticulously restored dovecote.
*Bailliffscourt**, Climping, West Sussex BN17 5RW. Telephone: 01903 723511. Website: www.hshotels.co.uk Hotel; dovecote older than house.
Basing House, Redbridge Lane, Old Basing, Hampshire RG24 7HB. Telephone: 01256 467294. Pair of dovecotes.
Beddington Park, Sutton, Surrey.
*Belcombe Court**, Bradford-on-Avon, Wiltshire.
Benthall Hall, Broseley, Shropshire TF12 5RX (NT). Telephone: 01952 582159.
*Blackford House Farm**, near Luccombe, Somerset. Early primitive stone dovecote with original domed roof and oculus. 1/4 mile south of A39 midway between Minehead and Porlock, signposted Luccombe.
*Blaise Hamlet**, Westbury-on-Trym, Bristol (NT). Telephone: 01985 843600. A pair of picturesque cottages with multiple gable nest holes.
Blockley, Gloucestershire. Small village; modern garage/dovecote. 5 miles south-east of Broadway off A44.
Breakspear House, Hillingdon, Middlesex.
Broughton, Hampshire. St Mary's churchyard.
Bruton, Somerset (NT). ST 684344. Impressive ruin of a sixteenth-century dovecote in a commanding position. Reached via A359 and Godminster Road.
*Chastleton House**, near Moreton-in-Marsh, Gloucestershire GL56 0SU (NT). Telephone: 01608 674355.
Chetwynd Park, near Newport, Shropshire. Octagonal brick dovecote seen from A41 one mile north of Newport.
Chicheley Hall, Chicheley, near Newport Pagnell, Buckinghamshire MK16 9JJ. Telephone: 01234 391252. Restored eighteenth-century octagonal brick dovecote.
Claremont Landscape Garden, Portsmouth Road, Esher, Surrey KT10 9JG (NT). Telephone: 01372 467806. A summerhouse converted back to a dovehouse.
Cliveden, Taplow, Maidenhead, Berkshire SL6 0JB (NT). Telephone: 01628 605069. Hotel; decorative dovecote in grounds.
Conisbrough Castle, Castle Hill, Conisbrough, Doncaster DN12 3BU (EH). Telephone: 01709 863329. Website: www.conisbroughcastle.org.uk SK 515989. 4 1/2 miles south-west of Doncaster off A1(M).
Cotehele House, St Dominick, Saltash, Cornwall PL12 6TA (NT). Telephone: 01579 350434.
Croxall Hall, Croxall, Staffordshire. Square red brick dovecote seen from the village street.
*Dunster**, Somerset. A classic dovecote beside the church.
*Eardisland**, Herefordshire. Telephone: 01544 288226. Restored 1999. Open to public. Exhibits.
Eastbury, Berkshire. Seen from the road, opposite Pigeon House.
Eastcote House, Pinner, Middlesex. In public garden.
*Erddig**, near Wrexham LL13 0YT (NT). Telephone: 01978 355314.
Felbrigg Hall, Felbrigg, Norwich, Norfolk NR11 8PR (NT). Telephone: 01263 837444.
Forcett Hall, Richmond, North Yorkshire. Newly restored.
*Glebe Farm**, Hill Croome, Upton upon Severn, Worcestershire. Restored by the Avoncroft Museum of Buildings.
Gunby Hall, Gunby, near Spilsby, Lincolnshire PE23 5SS (NT). Telephone: 01909 486411.
Hamstall Hall, Hamstall Ridware, Staffordshire. Ridware Arts Centre: important Tudor gateway containing nest holes.

*Hangleton Manor Hotel**, Hangleton, near Brighton, East Sussex. Telephone: 01273 413266. Restored flint and chalk dovecote.

Hawford Dovecote, Worcestershire (NT). SO 846607. 3 miles north of Worcester, 1/2 mile east of A449.

Hodnet Hall Gardens, near Market Drayton, Shropshire. Telephone: 01630 685202.

Hutton-in-the-Forest, Skelton, Cumbria. Telephone: 017684 84449. Estate open to public.

*Ightham Mote**, Sevenoaks, Kent (NT). Telephone: 01732 810378. Courtyard gatehouse.*

Kentwell Hall, Long Melford, Suffolk CO10 9BA. Telephone: 01787 310207. Square eighteenth-century dovecote. Open to public.

Kinwarton Dovecote, Warwickshire (NT). Telephone: 01684 855300. SP 106585. 1 1/2 miles north-east of Alcester, just south of B4089.

Low Middleton Hall, Middleton St George, County Durham. NZ 364059.

*Loxley Hall School**, Uttoxeter, Staffordshire. Visible from A518, 2 miles west of Uttoxeter.

*Luntley Court**, near Eardisland, Herefordshire. Miniature timber-framed dovecote.

Lytes Cary Manor, near Charlton Mackrell, Somerton, Somerset TA11 7HU (NT). Telephone: 01985 843600. Water pumphouse, ingeniously contrived to resemble a dovecote.

Manorbier Castle, near Pembroke, Pembrokeshire. Telephone: 01834 871394.

The Manor House, Rothersthorpe, Northamptonshire. Interesting nineteenth-century dovecote with low-pitched roof, seen from Rothersthorpe to Pattishall road.

Minster Lovell Hall and Dovecote, near Witney, Oxfordshire (EH). SP 324114. 12 miles west of Oxford just off A40.

Mitcham Dovecote, Canons Leisure Centre, Madeira Road, Mitcham, Surrey CR4 4HD. Early sixteenth-century square brick dovecote.

*Moat Farm**, Dormston, Worcestershire. SO 984573. Timber-framed pigeon house in the care of the Avoncroft Museum of Buildings.

Monks Risborough, near Princes Risborough, Buckinghamshire. SP 813045. Sixteenth-century stone dovecote near the church.

Motcombe Gardens, Eastbourne, East Sussex.

*Newtimber Place**, Newtimber, West Sussex BN6 9BU. Telephone: 01273 833104. Website: www.newtimber.co.uk

Norton St Philip, Somerset. Tudor dovecote, signposted in village.

*Norton sub Hamdon**, Somerset. Circular dovecote in St Mary's churchyard.

Nymans Garden, Handcross, near Haywards Heath, West Sussex RH17 6EB (NT). Telephone: 01444 400321.

*Painswick Rococo Garden**, Painswick, Gloucestershire GL6 6TH. Telephone: 01452 813204.

*Parham House**, Parham Park, near Pulborough, West Sussex RH20 4HS. Telephone: 01903 742021. Website: www.parhaminsussex.co.uk

Patcham, near Brighton, East Sussex. Interesting ancient dovecote.

Penmon Priory, Anglesey (CADW). North of Beaumaris off B5109.

*Pimp Hall**, Chingford, London E4. Restored, timber framed dovecote.

Rochester Castle, Rochester, Kent ME1 1SX (EH). Telephone: 01634 402276.

Rockingham Castle, near Corby, Northamptonshire. Telephone: 01536 770240. Dovecote within gateway bastion.

Rousham House, near Steeple Aston, Bicester, Oxfordshire OX6 3QX. Telephone: 01869 347110.

Shapwick House, Shapwick, Somerset TA7 9NL. Telephone: 01458 210321. In hotel grounds, exceptional hexagonal blue lias dovecote.

Sibthorpe, Nottinghamshire. St Mary's churchyard.

Snowshill Manor, near Broadway, Worcestershire WR12 7JU (NT). Telephone: 01386 852410.

Squerryes Court, Westerham, Kent TN16 1SJ. Telephone: 01959 562345.

Stoke sub Hamdon Priory, North Street, Stoke-sub-Hamdon, Somerset TA4 6QP (NT). Telephone: 01985 843600. Building under restoration.

*Sulham**, near Reading, Berkshire. Folly/dovecote can be seen from eastbound carriageway of M4 just before Junction 12; take this exit for access.

Thame, Oxfordshire. St Mary's churchyard.

Whitehall, Monkmoor Road, Shrewsbury, Shropshire. Fine dovecote in car park of modern local municipal offices.

*Wichenford Dovecote**, Worcestershire (NT). Telephone: 01684 855300. SO 788597. 5 1/2 miles north-west of Worcester off B4204.

*Willington Dovecote and Stables**, Willington, Bedfordshire (NT). Telephone: 01494 528051. TL 107499. Very unusual; it resembles some Scottish and French dovecotes.

*Witton Castle**, Witton-le-Wear, County Durham DL14 0DE. Telephone: 01388 488230.

Wollaton Hall, Nottingham NG8 2AE. Telephone: 0115 915 3900. Has dovecote as part of courtyard complex. Exhibits.

Wytham, Oxfordshire. Fine dovecote in car park of the White Hart public house.